The Foundation of Truth
Part 1

Understanding The Apostles' Teaching
Adam and Eve In Pursuit of the
Knowledge of Good and Evil
to become wise as God

By Bishop Wilfred Brown, JP

Order this book online at www.trafford.com
or email orders@trafford.com

Most Trafford titles are also available at major online book retailers.

Printed in the United States of America.

ISBN: 978-1-4907-3769-0 (sc)
ISBN: 978-1-4907-3771-3 (hc)
ISBN: 978-1-4907-3770-6 (e)

Library of Congress Control Number: 2014909743

Trafford rev.   05/28/2014

North America & international
toll-free: 1 888 232 4444 (USA & Canada)
fax: 812 355 4082

A Guide to All Believers of the Faith

Of Jesus Christ

The Apostolic Perspective

Author: Bishop Wilfred M. Brown

Prepared by Bishop Wilfred M. Brown
Prelate/Founder of
The International Assembly of Apostolic
Believers Evangelistic Association
Incorporated 1985
Email: bishopbrown692@gmail.com
Tel: 876-855-2627

CONTENTS

		Page
Preface		8
Chapter 1	The futile attempts and Vain Imaginations of Adam and Eve	9
Chapter 2	The words of deception by the serpent to make Adam and Eve wise	11
	Adam and Eve in the Garden of Eden	11
Chapter 3	The danger of sin and its consequences	17
Chapter 4	The call by God to Abraham; his perfect choice	20
	Israel and the church to celebrate the Passover (Lord's Supper)	22
	Circumcision by the Spirit required in the New Testament Church	24
	The awareness of our pursuits	25
Chapter 5	Abraham foresees Israel's affliction as a horror of great darkness	30
Chapter 6	The awesome appearance of the Glory of God to Moses	32
Chapter 7	The guaranteed words of Jesus	38
Chapter 8	The unfolding of the wisdom of God	40
	The Sons of God shall always be led by the Spirit of God	42
Chapter 9	Serving God with the mind of Christ	43
Chapter 10	Lord Jesus the exalted name, the only saving name	45

Chapter 11   The Testimony of Jesus is the   46
              spirit of prophecy

Chapter 12   The Lord's purpose for His call   47
              to the nation and to Israel

Chapter 13   God in Jesus Christ; the Unique One   48
              No man hath seen God at any time: 48
              Murmurings and disputes are forbidden   49

Chapter 14   Believing the of Gospel of Christ brings,   50
              the Righteousness which is of God by faith

Chapter 15   Jesus the Author and Finisher of   51
              our faith, in Whom God first trusted
              Jesus, the gift of God to the world   52
              The prophecy concerning Christ   52

Chapter 16   The mystery of the Gospel revealed   55
              to Paul
              Christ the Power of God and the   56
              Wisdom of God

Chapter 17   God's Proclamation fulfilled in   57
              Jesus Christ
              The prayer of Jerimiah to God: 58
              The promise of the new covenant
              of keeping mercy foretold: 58
              The soul of unrepentant sinners
              is sick and needs healing: 60

Chapter 18   Christ Jesus the Suffering Servant   60
              We are commanded to take the Gospel
              unto the uttermost part of the earth:
              Acts 1: 8.   61

This book on Adam and Eve and their pursuit for the knowledge of good and evil with its effects on their lives, subsequent to their action as well as the entire human race, is hereby outlined with its consequence to explain to the reader of this book the importance of obedience and the devastating effects their disobedience brought on themselves and all the human family created after the same similitude.

It shows the three phases of the commands of God from the Garden of Eden , to Israel at Mt. Sanai,to the giving of the law of the spirit of life in Christ Jesus which hath made us free from the law of sin and death (the Ten Commandments).

The law given to Israel goes hand in hand with sin and death, because failure to obey the law brings its consequences. For by the deeds of the law there shall no flesh (human) be justified in God's sight: for by the law is the knowledge of sin. Therefore, by faith in Jesus Christ, all flesh shall be justified or declared righteous in God's sight.

CHAPTER 1

The Futile Attempt and Vain Imagination
of Adam and Eve

In the book of Genesis, the book of the beginning of the creation of God, it is recorded that God created the heaven and the earth and all things therein by the word of His power. Then God blessed all of the creatures that He made, saying: "Be fruitful and multiply". That is, everything that flies in the firmament of the heavens, every living thing that moves in the waters, and those things in the earth. God said "Let the earth bring forth the living creature after his kind" and it was so. Thus, God saw that all that He made was good. See Gen. 1:1-25 After which God said "Let us make man in our image (character), after our likeness: And let them have dominion over the fish of the sea, and over the fowl of the air, and over the cattle, and over all the earth, and over every creeping thing that creepeth upon the earth.

So God created man in His own image. In the image of God created He him; male and female created He them. And God blessed them, and God said unto them, "Be fruitful, and multiply, and replenish (Fill up) the earth, and subdue it: And have dominion over the fish of the sea, and over the fowl of the air, and over every living thing that moveth upon the earth. (Gen. 1:24-28).

As it is shown, Adam and Eve were given complete authority to have control over all the earthly creatures and to replenish (fill up) the earth. They were both well favoured by God, being made in His own image and likeness and treated as one flesh.

Adam was greatly respected by God in that, Adam was given the opportunity to name every living creature that God had made, including Eve, the mother of the whole human family, his wife, and in God's sight they were one flesh because she was taken from Adam, to cleave to each other. For God had said husband and wife shall leave Father and Mother and cleave to each other. In using the example of Adam and Eve see Gen. 2:18, 21-24.

As a result of man's wonderful creation by God, including the entire universe that He has made, the Psalmist, in his assessment and reflection of the greatness of God and His wonderful works which He did, declared: I will praise Thee (in his expression of gratitude), for I am fearfully and wonderfully made. Marvelous are Thy works, and that my soul (self) knoweth right well. My substance was not hidden from Thee, when I was made in secret and curiously (intricately) wrought in the lowest parts of the earth, Ps 139:14-15.

Such were the thinking and expressions of David, as he thought of God's great blessings that were bestowed upon mankind. Having the divine nature of God within them and possessed with eternal life, thus enabling them to have constant fellowship with God, having the ability before the fall to reason and to think right, so that all the creatures that Adam had named were accepted by God, because the Spirit of God was endued within him so that he could name them right.

However, there was a creature called the serpent which God had created, and it was more subtle (cunning) than any beast of the field which the Lord God had made, which appeared to Eve in the garden of Eden.

This creature had given itself to Satan. It should be noted that this beast, in its first creation, was not a writhing reptile or snake that crept on its belly until it was cursed by God for the part it played in the fall of man.

This beast was used as an agent of the devil which

had envied Adam and Eve for the dominion they were given by God over the entire earth, and in the seas, to execute their authority.

For this reason he cunningly beguiled Eve and twisted the Word of God concerning the tree of knowledge of good and evil. Then Eve hearkened to the devil's lie and was deceived, which resulted in their transgression and subsequent spiritual and physical death, as well as all the consequences of sin, pain, sickness, child bearing with pain, labour with difficulties and all the causes of sin by their disobedience.

Thus, Satan tried to usurp God's authority on the earth as shown in his futile attempt to tempt the Lord Jesus in His forty days and forty nights fasting in the wilderness. Mt. 4:5-9

CHAPTER 2

The words of deception by the serpent to make Adam & Eve wise as God

The words of deception spoken by the serpent which misled Adam and Eve, that they would be wise as God, is the most deceptive of all deceptions, and cunning, which worked in their minds, "ye shall not surely die".

That statement from the serpent, that their eyes shall be opened and that they shall be wise as gods, knowing good and evil, brought their downfall. That disobedient response to God's command shows that we should be careful to what we give ourselves to hear, and what we are in agreement with. This account of that incident shows that it is foolish to think that we can be as wise as God, who created us with all His manifold wisdom, power and all other attributes vested in Him.

Adam and Eve in the Garden of Eden

This was the sole purpose when it appeared to Eve in the garden of Eden. To dethrone them of their dominion given to them by God. Thus the serpent said to Eve, "Yea hath God said ye shall not eat of every tree of the garden?" And the woman said unto the serpent, "We may eat of the fruit of the trees of the garden. But of the fruit of the tree which is in the midst of the garden, God hath said, ye shall not eat of it, neither shall ye touch it, lest ye die." And the serpent said unto the woman, "Ye shall not surely die, for God doth know that in the day ye eat thereof, then your eyes shall be opened, and ye shall be as gods (God), knowing good and evil."

Thoughts of those kinds are vain imagination which leads to negative behaviour that will lead us astray from God and ultimately His blessings, He has promised for our faithfulness and obedience to do His will.

The commands He gives are positive. They are given for upliftment in our lives. Those thoughts we should inculcate in our minds. They are Christ-like and they are positive thinking which will bring to us our heavenly rewards. Thus, deception and false beliefs outside of God's commands, was an evil seed sown and conceived into the heart of Eve and Adam, grown into an evil fruit of a false concept that she could become wise as God, knowing good and evil.

Thus she engaged her heart with the urge to be wise as God. She developed pride to be as God, with great wisdom and power to live forever and not die.

This idea in mind was born out of the word of deception and falsehood sown in her heart by the serpent. With that thought in her mind, she had seen the tree as pleasant to the eyes, and a tree to be desired to make one wise. She took of the fruit thereof, and did eat, and gave also unto her husband with her, and he did eat. See Gen. 3:1-7. In one way or another, mankind shall be always seeking to obtain knowledge of something he desires and regards as important to his wellbeing.

However, for this to be attainable, the fear of God is vital, thus showing reverence to God in the spirit of obedience which is the principal thing. In that we are aware that our Creator is great in might and awesome in power to be reverenced. Ps. 95:3-11, Ps. 111:7-10. This will be so because whenever we think about God it is natural for our thoughts to go back to the creation of the universe, as well as our own creation.

Man's reflection of God is towards the Almighty who is self exist, eternal and infinite, without beginning of days nor end of days. Therefore, by this understanding, when God made Adam and Eve, they were well aware of God's great power and wisdom in whom eternal life is embodied, and Him only life is given and by Him life is taken. Therefore by this acknowledgement of Adam and Eve, they were given the sternest command throughout human history, which would determine life or death, blessing and cursing upon the entire human race, which had set the condition for grace and divine judgment by God alone.

Consequently God showed them the tree of knowledge of good and evil for them to make their choice either to live or die. However, unfortunately, they chose death by their action, rather than to keep life. The devil's attempt to derail God's eternal plan of life everlasting: Gen. 2:15-17; Gen. 3:4

Adam and Eve, the first human parents, were particularly blessed, being made directly by the precious and holy hands of God, who made them in His own image and likeness with the divine character of holiness which formed their natural and spiritual life, and as a result of this quality by which they were made they were endowed or furnished with the covering of the glory of God. Thus they did not know they were naked, because God's glory was their clothing and by this creation, they pleased God, consequently His finished work was all good in His sight.

As a result of this quality of life Adam and Eve enjoyed life in its fullness. Satan moved with covetous-ness to stop that quality of life, to have them stripped of God's glory and covering, permanently to make them naked with the consequence of sin to follow. Hence, Sa-tan's attempt to stop God's eternal plan of everlasting life with His earthly creation of human beings. Therefore, on this basis, man's character was put to the test by God to determine the choice Adam and Eve would make between obedience to God's word of truth and the devil's guile and deception.

This was man's great test to prove his direction for his future. The reflection of life given to Adam and Eve, was dependent on them solely to observe God's word in strict obedience in all His commands. This was the condition laid down by God to them, that is, to abide in all things commanded of them. God gave to Adam the specifics to maintain life. Gen. 2:7-9, 17.

We do not know how long after Adam and Eve were created that they were given God's solemn command to keep. But we know according to the scripture God gave them, His warning, after He planted a garden eastward in Eden, and there He put the man whom He had formed. And out of the ground made the Lord God to grow every tree that was pleasant to the sight, and good for food; the tree of life also in the midst of the garden, and the tree of knowledge of good and evil.

All the trees were pleasant to the sight and good for food. But God made special emphasis of the forbidden tree of knowledge of good and evil. This dual natured fruit had in it two distinct substances of two different flavours and nutrients that would be good in part but harmful in its other mixture to the human sense and soul. Hence it was forbidden by God to eat of it. Gen. 2:8-9. It was God's divine act to make this fruit part good and part evil. In the book of Isaiah, the prophet wrote about God's divine act saying "I form light and create darkness. I make peace and create evil or calamity; I the Lord do all these things." Isa. 45:7. See Isa. 31:1-2; Isa. 47:8-11.

Concerning Jacob and Esau, Paul wrote; It was said unto her, that is Rebecca, the elder shall serve the younger. As it is written, Jacob have I loved, but Esau have I hated. What shall we say then? Is there unrighteousness with God? God forbid. Rom. 9: 12-14.

So then, for the children being not yet born, neither having done any good or evil, that the purpose of God, according to election, might stand not of works, but of him that calleth. Rom. 9:11. This was God's purpose foretold of beforehand, indicating the election that it is of God who calls us and not of our works. It was God's divine acts to save both Jews and Gentiles.

The apostle attributed this to the depth of the riques both of the wisdom and Knowledge of God. In describing this quality of God he says: How unsearchable are his judgments, meaning his decisions, and his ways past finding out: For who hath known the mind of the Lord? Or who hath been his counsellor? See Rom. 11: 30 -34.

As we have seen through the scriptures that God's divine purpose cannot be fathomed by our fallible minds. Therefore the essential thing to do, to please God, is to heed the counsel of the preacher as he has given instruction. Let us hear the conclusion of the whole matter: Fear God, and keep His commandments: for this is the whole duty of man. See Eccl. 12:13

CHAPTER 3

The danger of sin and its consequence

Before sin is conceived, it is presented in a manner that seems good to the eyes (Gen. 3: 5-6), but it is false, and if the deception is accepted within the mind, and the heart, and it is conceived, the consequence is death spiritually (Jas. 1:13-15), followed by physical death.

This was the case with Adam and Eve. The devil presented a false reply to the truth of God's word and it seemed good in the mind of Eve.

Hence she was deceived (1 Tim. 2:14). Then Adam hearkened to Eve when she presented it (the fruit of good and evil) and they both fell into the transgression (Gen. 3: 16-19). Thus the consequence of sin is very great and costly (Ps. 49: 7-8).

This was the result of Adam and Eve, in that, when they were both created they were not ashamed, because they did not know they were naked. (Gen. 2:25). They were able to stand in the presence of God, and commune with Him. See Gen. 3:8-9; Job 38: 1; Ex. 19: 17-18 Ezek. 1: 3-4. The feelings of guilt came because of their disobedience to God's command, and as a result they felt afraid of God.

Therefore they hid themselves knowing they were naked. The knowledge of evil which they possessed after they ate of the tree of knowledge of good and evil brought about their knowledge of sin and the awareness of its consequences. See Gen. 3: 6-7, 10-11.

It was evident that Adam and Eve had the pleasure and privilege to meet with God at various times. Therefore, at His usual time, the Lord called unto Adam, and said unto him, where art thou? Adam said to God, I heard thy voice in the garden, and was afraid because I was naked.

Sin had brought onto Adam his separation from God, and therefore he could not stand in the presence of God's glory anymore. This will be the result of all those who have fallen from God's standard of holiness, and uprightness. They were brought to a lower state by their own failure through the undesirable knowledge of evil they had possessed, because of their sin.

Adam and Eve began to experience a new way of lifestyle which did not bring them happiness anymore, and God's glory departed from them. Their eyes were opened to a lifestyle that was worse than before, which their disobedient action brought upon them and they were driven out of the garden of Eden, Scripture reference Gen. 3: 23-24.

Their new experience brought hardship through labour, thorns and thistles, by the sweat of their face, they would toil for the produce from the earth, which all mankind would experience through their labour: Also Eve was told she would experience sorrow through child bearing and subsequently their life would be given a time limit by physical death and they would return to the earth from whence they came, Gen. 3:19.

However, God's mercy from everlasting to everlasting, according to His own divine nature and character, was manifested. Therefore: Moses the man of God proclaimed: The Lord, the Lord God, merciful and gracious, long-suffering, (forbearing and patient with mankind), and abundant in goodness and truth. Keeping mercy for the thousands, forgiving iniquity and transgression and sin, and that will by no means clear the guilty; visiting the iniquity of the fathers upon the children's children unto the third and the forth generation, Ex. 34: 6-7.

Now when Adam and Eve had sinned, the eyes of them both had opened (by their knowledge of evil), and they knew that they were naked, and they sewed fig leaves together, and made themselves aprons, and subsequently did the Lord God make coats of skins, and clothed them. God was demonstrating His mercy towards mankind from that instance and throughout the generations that would follow.

God displayed His patience and mercy towards mankind when they had forsaken His command, to obtain knowledge of good and evil by their vain imagination and committed sin in that effort, which led to their expulsion and death by sin. Therefore, man's pursuit of knowledge by disobeying God's command or His law, is the knowledge of sin and the breaking of God's law. Thus, the first sin was to violate, or to overpass God's law or rule prescribed to Adam and Eve in the garden of Eden. As apostle John tells us: for sin is the transgression of the law. 1 John 3: 4. Because the law worketh wrath: For where no law is, there is no transgression. Rom. 4: 15.

Man's first step in exploring knowledge by the law of God was in the garden of Eden, where he was commanded not to seek after the knowledge of good versus evil.

Since the law of God worketh wrath, then His laws demands absolute obedience or strict adherence, and failure to abide will result in committing sin. See Gal. 3:10, 19: Rom. 7:8, 10-11; 1 John 3:4. For as by one man's disobedience many were made sinners, so by the obedience of one Christ Jesus, shall many be made right-eous. Moreover the law entered, that the offence might abound. But where sin abounded, grace did much more abound, Rom. 5:19-20.

God's foreknowledge of all things, and His righteous provision by His grace, was key to establishing
man's deliverance in every age. For whom He did fore-
know, He also did predestine to be conformed to the
image of His Son, that he might be the firstborn among
many brethren, Rom. 8:29.

CHAPTER 4

The call by God to Abraham the perfect choice: Gen. 12:1-3

The call by God to Abraham manifests His
purpose for the election and justification by faith through
which righteousness is accounted, Rom. 4:5-6. Therefore
his calling gives us the source of the family roots of the
people of God, through which God would use as the
spiritual channel of obedience, faith, righteousness and
love unfeigned from a true heart. (Acts 3:25, Gal. 3:29).

The foundation or source of origin of building a
spiritual family is critical. Therefore in God's divine plan
starting with Abraham was the ideal election of choice.
Thus, God in His foreknowledge, knew that Abraham
would be the best choice in beginning the new generation
of righteous people after the flood. Hence God's call to
Abram was perfect. Gen. 12:1-4.

The blessings of obedience:

The Lord's promise to Abraham for his obedience states: I
will bless them that bless thee, and curse him that curseth
thee: and in thee shall all the families of the earth be
blessed. So Abraham departed, as the Lord had spoken
unto him: and Lot went with him: And A'bram was sev-

enty and five years old when he departed out of Haran, Gen. 12:3-4.

Therefore the call by God to A'bram (as he was called) was the perfect and true test. Gen. 12:1-4. The test of faith and obedience which leads to the everlasting promise. Josh. 24:1-3. Stephen's testimony and defense affirmed the faith and obedience of Abraham to his own brethren. Acts 7:1-8. As well as the testimony of the "Heroes", of faith. Where it is mentioned: By faith Abraham, when he was called to go out into a place which he should after receive for an inheritance, obeyed, and he went out, not knowing where he was going. Thus, by faith he sojourned in the land of promise, as in a strange or foreign country, dwelling in tabernacles, with Isaac and Jacob, the heirs with him of the same promise: For he looked (was waiting) for a city which had foundations, whose builder and maker is God, Heb. 11:8-10.

This call to Abraham for obedience and faith was the real challenge Abraham faced to prove himself, in the first instance by God, which he did and thereby qualified himself for the blessings of God for his entire life, through the promise made to him. As God himself made promise to Abraham saying: I will make of thee a great nation: (Gen. 17:6; Gen. 18:18; Deut. 26:5; Hos. 12:12-13.) In thee shall all the families of the earth be blessed, Gen. 18:18; Gen. 22:18; Gen. 26:4; Ps. 72:17; Acts 25; Gal. 3:18. Thus, Israel's blessings the result of their deliverance by the prophets, sent by God: These blessings foretold of to Abraham, were calculated to be executed by Israel's deliverance through the prophets sent to Egypt by God to take them out of the house of bondage to the promised land. Ex. 3:1-10.

Jacob, who is called Israel, had fled into the country of Syria (Gen. 28:1-5), and Israel served for a wife, and for a wife he kept sheep. And by a prophet the Lord brought Israel out of Egypt, and by a prophet was he preserved (Hos. 12:12-13)

Israel and the church to celebrate the Passover (Lord's Supper)

The ordinance of the Passover observed before Israel left Egypt: Then the Lord said unto Moses and Aaron, This is the ordinance of the Passover: There shall no stranger eat thereof: But every man's servant that is bought for money, when thou hast circumcised him, then shall he eat thereof. A foreigner and a hired servant shall not eat thereof.

In one house shall it (the Passover) be eaten; thou shalt not carry forth aught (any) of the flesh abroad out of the house; neither shall ye break a bone thereof. All the congregation of Israel shall keep it. And when a stranger shall sojourn with thee, and will keep the Passover to the Lord, let all his males be circumcised, and then let him come near and keep it; and he shall be as one that is born in the land; For no uncircumcised person shall eat thereof.

One law (rule or tenet) shall be to him that is home born, and unto the stranger that sojourneth among you. Thus did all the children of Israel, as the Lord commanded Moses and Aaron, so did they. And it came to pass the selfsame day, that the Lord brought the children of Israel out of the land of Egypt by their armies. Ex. 12:43-51.

Israel and the church to celebrate the Passover:

Moses, whom God had sent to Egypt to deliver Israel from their bondage, reminded them after they had ate the Passover which was their last day there, said they should remember this (that) day, in which they came out from Egypt, out of the house of bondage (slaves); for by strength of hand the Lord brought them out from this (that) place: <u>There shall be no leavened bread be eaten this (that) day came ye out in the month of Abib.</u> (April).

The Passover should be kept a memorial feast at evening: Ex. 12:1-6, 14:17-18. This memorial feast was observed by all Israel throughout the Old Testament period as the Lord commanded. All the persons who had kept the feast (Passover) had to be circumcised: Gen. 17:9-11, 23-27, Rom. 4:11.

The significance of circumcision is: it is a commandment from the Lord and a covenant between the individual, the nation and God.

Circumcision by the Spirit required in the New Testament Church

Apostle Paul revealed its purpose by explaining Abraham's circumcision: He told us, "Abraham received the sign of circumcision, a seal of the righteousness of the faith" which he had, yet being uncircumcised: That he might be the father of all them (Jews and Gentiles) that believe, though they be not circumcised: That righteousness might be imputed or accounted unto them (the uncircumcised also). Rom. 4: 11.

Circumcision represents the cutting off, of the flesh, and the cutting off, of our connection with the world. Circumcision by the spirit is required in the New Testament church: See Rom. 2: 29.

The Apostle Paul has shown that the method of circumcision under the first covenant prescribed by the letter, is finished, and a new application has been instituted by the Spirit of God. Paul, in showing the difference between the operation of the flesh and the spirit, indicates: That a Jew is not one which is one outwardly; neither is that circumcision, which is outward in the flesh: As previously done. See (Gen. 17: 9-11, Ex. 4: 22-26).

Spiritual circumcision instituted:

But he is a Jew, which is one inwardly (that is, spiritually done): Thus circumcision is one of the heart, (the hidden man of the heart, in that which is not corruptible, even the ornament of a meek and quiet spirit 1 Pet. 3: 4) the characteristics of a Jew. For we are the circumcision, which worship God in the Spirit, and rejoice in Christ Jesus, and have no confidence in the flesh, Phil. 3: 3.

Therefore circumcision is that of the heart in the spirit, which requires the worshiper to worship God in the Spirit (Deut. 30: 6; 1 Cor. 4: 5), and not in the letter, whose praise (1 Pet. 2:9) is not of men, but of God. Rom. 2: 28-29. As a result we judge nothing before the time (For the final praise), until the Lord returns, who both will bring to light (into evidence) the hidden things of darkness (Mt. 10: 26), and will make manifest the counsels (motives) of the hearts. And then shall every man have praise of God, 1 Cor. 4: 5. The disclosure of the hearts will be made known as in the case of the Samaritan woman, John 4: 16-18, 28. Who said: Come, see a man, which told me all things that I ever did: Is not this (would this he) the Christ? John 4: 29. Then they of the city came unto him, John 4: 30.

His revelation will bring to light the hidden man of the heart, and then shall all men see what is the mystery of Christ, hidden in the fleshy table of the heart. Then shall we give Him praise as they, in the city of Samaria, John 4: 30.

The awareness of our pursuits:

The awareness of our pursuits in life are key factors to determine the way forward for a successful life and a blessed outcome. Therefore knowledge is imperative in all our pursuits. This is why Adam and Eve were well informed about the tree of knowledge of good and evil. Thus, the fruit from this particular tree had changed Adam and Eve into persons possessing different characteristics from their original creation, being embodied with good and evil giving birth to sin and its evil nature.

It is therefore reasonable to conclude that we can be unaware of the result of our pursuits in life without prior knowledge.

That is why Adam and Eve were properly informed about the tree of knowledge of good and evil by God who made the tree in that manner.

So that they would be accountable for their actions, which they pursued and failed because they had disobeyed God's command given to them.

The Precepts of God Given to All mankind:

The precepts of God given to all mankind are the rules that are stipulated by God for good order in the realm of His Kingdom.

In keeping these rules intact we <u>shall demonstrate or accomplish</u> the virtues of the Lord's prayer which He taught His disciples to transfer godliness on earth as it is in heaven.

Therefore loyalty to God is very essential for His precepts to be honoured consequently to dishonor the

Lord's prayer is to refuse the right of His authority to pray or bow down before God. The first violation of God's rule, was done by Lucifer in heaven which followed his expulsion from God's holy habitation. See Isa. 14: 9-15; Ezek. 28: 2, 6, 14-19.

That is why when God placed Adam and Eve in the Garden of Eden they were given strict instructions what they should do and should not do. Therefore they were given a choice to determine their future for eternity.

The pursuit of knowledge to possess Life in God:

The pursuit of knowledge is to remain true to the commands of God and continuing in the path that God places us. Constantly following in His steps abiding always in His counsel, which is to be obedient to Him the only true God who is vested with eternal life.

Doing God's will and delighting ourselves in His word will be the prerequisite in maintaining the true state of God's Kingdom on earth (Rom. 14: 17-18) bringing glory to His name and Lordship, displaying the honour due unto Him in holy adoration to His authority.

Keeping the fellowship and endeavouring to keep the unity of the Spirit of God making the communion ongoing on earth as it is in heaven as recorded in the Lord's prayer to His disciples, Mt. 6: 9-13.

The Pursuit of God's Wisdom among wen:

God intended for us to be wise as His creatures made after His image or character and His likeness that is, His similitude to be like Him in the person of Christ Jesus (1 John 3: 2.) As the Apostle Paul tells us: let this mind be in you which was also in Christ Jesus. Who, being in the form of God, thought it not robbery to be equal with God. Which means as children of God, born from Him that is from above, spiritually adopted in the family of God. See scripture references: Phil. 2: 5-6; John 3: 3-5; Gal. 4: 4-6.

Believers who are born again are expected to portray His wisdom staying in the course He has designed for us in His righteous counsel.

The Purpose of Christ Jesus coming to the earth:

Adam the first recipient of God made human is of the earth, and therefore was earthly in nature and conduct. But Christ Jesus, who came from above is above all. Which were born, not of blood, nor of the will of the flesh, neither of the will of man, that is, of human intention or ability of man, but of God.

The first man Adam, his thinking is of the earth and as a result his reasoning and speech had human connotation in his utterances and motives, were earthly.

But he that comes from heaven, who is Christ Jesus is above all humanity. He is the second man, the Lord from heaven. Christ Jesus who came to earth exclusively to accomplish the purpose which Adam who pre-figured the Lord Jesus came to do, but failed in His effort.   So as Adam was of the earth and earthy, that is, in conduct. Such are they also that are earthy of the same ilk or type.

Conforming to the Image of Christ on Earth:

Comparatively,   Adam's life was similar in nature and conduct to all earthy mortals of the same and there is no difference in that respect. Acts 17: 26

The precedence has been prescribed for all humanity by the appearance of the coming of Christ Jesus regarding His earthly life style during His time on earth. For us to pattern for orderly and acceptable standard of living (Luke 1: 71-75) before God.

Therefore if we bear the image of the life of Christ Jesus while He was on earth in flesh (2 Cor. 5: 16) We shall also bear the image (immortality) of the heavenly, 1 Cor. 15: 49. See 2 Cor. 3: 18.

This criteria was stipulated bt God for the failure of Adam in the Garden of Eden. See Rom. 5: 12-15. For this cause the Apostle Paul, asserted: Now this I say: Brethren, that flesh and blood cannot inherit the Kingdom of God; neither doth corruption inherit incorruption. 1 Cor. 15: 50.

The Wise Shall Inherit Glory:

It is recorded, the path of the just (righteous) is as the shining light, that shineth more and more unto the perfect day, Prov. 4: 18. The path the righteous takes, represents Christ's life which was the true light that lighteth everyone that comes into the world.

Of such Christ Jesus, characterizes His disciples as a city that is set on a hill cannot be hid. Therefore the life of the righteous represents the true life of Christ and these are the symbols of transformation from the darkness of sinful living to the path of righteous living which shall continue to shine perpetual until the perfect day when Christ returns, 1 Thess. 4: 15-18.

The Wise Shall Inherit Immortality:

This will be the ultimate blessing of the wise in manifesting the glory of God with the new body of immortality.

This special moment is imminent and is approaching very fast: For the earth shall be filled with the knowledge of the glory of the Lord, as the waters cover the sea, Hab. 2: 14.

Immortality shall be the final phase of the heavenly bliss, to bring glory to the wise, the faithful and the righteous in Christ Jesus: The second man, the Lord from heaven, the last Adam, made a quickening spirit.

He will be returning for the born again (John 3: 3, 5). For the Apostle Paul, affirmed, saying: Behold, I show you a mystery (secret); we shall not all sleep (in death, at His appearing), but we shall be changed. In a moment, in the twinkling of an eye, at the last trump: For the trumpet shall sound, and the dead shall be raised incorruptible, and we shall be changed, 1 Cor. 15: 51-52. See also 2 Cor. 5: 1-2, 4.

The moment that we are all anticipating, which is certain is at hand, let's be prepared fully, be steadfast in your patience. Our joy then shall be full and complete, when we shall be in His likeness. Peace!

CHAPTER 5

Abraham foresees Israel's affliction as an horror of great darkness

The prophecy concerning Israel's bondage and affliction was revealed to him in a vision while he was at Canaan, the land of promise, after he had left Ur of the Chaldea's, the homeland of his father, Terah's nativity, Gen 11: 27, while he sojourned in Canaan at the command of God. The Lord said to Abraham in a vision: Know of a surety that thy seed shall be a stranger in a land that is not theirs, and shall serve them, and they shall afflict them four hundred years. And also that nation, whom they shall serve, will I judge and afterward shall they come out with great substances or possessions, Gen. 15: 12-14.

The affliction Israel endured in Egypt during their sojourn, as foreseen by Abraham, was an experience described as an horror of great darkness. Horror, connotes a feeling of fear, dread and abhorrence. The horror of darkness was great misery experienced by the children of

Israel. They had no idea if light would come their way in their dark period of sojourn which lasted four hundred and thirty years of bondage. See Ex.12: 40.

God's divine intervention and deliverance from the bondage of sin, and from Satan of both Jews and Gentiles, to receive eternal life in Jesus Christ, justifies the exhortation of the psalmist to Israel, as well as to the whole world, to praise the name of the Lord Jesus from the rising of the sun unto the going down of the same. The prophet in foretelling God's redemptive plan prophesied that His name shall be great among the Gentiles (the nations of the world); and in every place incense, the offering up of prayers shall be constantly going up to God as a pleasing, sweet-smelling odour, and a pure offering to the one true God for His name is great among the heathens. (Mal. 1: 11)

Refusal to be on the Lord's side is to reject the principal thing which is wisdom and that is to fear God. (Prov. 4: 7; Mt. 13: 41-44; Prov. 1: 17).

The prophet Jerimiah's counsel to Israel to be secured with God says: Let not the wise man glory in his wisdom, neither let the mighty man glory in his riches: But let him that glorieth glory in this, that he understandeth and knoweth Me, that I am the Lord which exercise loving kindness , judgment and righteousness, in the earth: For in these things I delight, saith the Lord. Jer. 9: 23-24.

CHAPTER 6

God's assurance to His people:

For thou art a holy people unto the Lord thy God: The Lord thy God has chosen thee to be a special people unto Himself, above all people that are upon the face of the earth.

The Lord did not set His love upon you (speaking of Israel), or had chosen you because ye were more in number than any people. For ye were the fewest of all people: But because the Lord loved you, and because He would keep the oath which He had sworn unto your fathers, hath the Lord brought you out with a mighty hand, and redeemed you out of bondage (slavery), from the hand of Pharaoh, king of Egypt. Deut. 7:6-8.

God is not partial in His first choice Israel. See Rom. 9: 8-14, 15-24. For He saith to Moses, I will have mercy on whom I will have mercy, and I will have compassion on whom I will have compassion. So then it is not on him that willeth, nor of him that runneth, but of God that showeth mercy.

We are all obliged to accept God's design plan of salvation in working out His purpose to bring both the vessels of wrath and the vessels of mercy into the same body, the church, of which Jesus Christ is Lord. It is to God's credit that we the vessels of wrath, fitted or prepared for destruction, have received mercy through Christ Jesus, and have become the vessels of honour.

Because by the riches of God's glory, which is Jesus our Lord, we have inherited all spiritual blessings in heavenly places. Having received His divine nature and are now complete in Him because of His fullness have we received springs of grace.

The unfolding of that great event by God, to bring about Israel's deliverance to the wilderness, where they started their next sojourn, and there they received the law of God as a nation corporately, to know God's requirements for them and to discover man's hidden sin, in their mortal being.

This was man's next test to please God, to do what the commandments say, to teach him to reject evil that was embodied in him, after the fall of man and to bring himself under subjection to do good. This was the purpose of the law. As the apostle Paul revealed to the Hebrews about the true meaning of the law, says: For the law having a shadow of good things to come, and not the very image of the things, can never with those sacrifices which they offered year by year continually make the comers thereunto perfect, Heb. 10: 1.

The Commandment encourages the mind to do well, but was ineffective in its outcome. See Rom. 7: 1-3; Rom. 8: 2. Wherefore, my brethren the Apostle encourages. ye also are become dead to the law (Gal. 2: 19; Rom. 6: 14; Gal. 5: 18; Eph. 2: 15; Col. 2: 14) by the body of Christ: that ye should be married to another (Rom. 7: 1-3), even to him who is raised from the dead, that ye should bring forth fruit unto God (Gal. 5: 22-25) for when we were in the flesh (outside of Christ), the motions (passions) of sins, which were by the law, did work in our members (bodies) to bring forth fruit unto death.

But now we are delivered from the law, that being dead wherein we were held (Rom. 6: 3-4; Rom. 7: 1-3); that we should serve in newness of spirit, and not in the oldness of the letter, Rom. 7: 4-6.

Our conversion, the result of God's great love: From spiritual death, to spiritual life in Jesus Christ. As the Apostle declared: And you hath he quickened (made alive), who were dead (spiritually) in trespasses and sins; Wherein in time past ye walked (lived a life dominated by the desires of our lower nature), according to the course of this world, according to the prince of the power of the air, the spirit that now worketh in the children of disobedience. Among whom also we all had our conversation (conduct) in times past in the lusts of our flesh and of the mind; and were by nature the children of wrath, even as others. But God, who is rich in mercy, for His great love wherewith He loved us. Even when we were dead in sins, hath quickened us together with Christ, by grace we are saved. And hath raised us up together, and made us sit together in heavenly places in Christ Jesus: That in the ages to come He might show the exceeding riches of His grace in His kindness toward us through Christ Jesus. For by grace are ye saved through faith; and that not of ourselves: it is the gift of God: Eph. 2: 1-8.

The law was our schoolmaster to bring us to Christ: Gal 3: 24. See Gal. 3: 6-10, 13-14, 17-18, 22-24, 25-27; Rom 5: 10-14; Rom. 3: 19-20; Rom. 7: 7, 14-24; Tim. 1: 9-16; Rom. 10: 1-4; Mt. 5: 17. The law was designed to silence all mankind under the conviction that they have nothing to say against the charge of sin.

Likewise, the law was intended to convince all men of their guilt, or liability to punishment, before God. The law assigns to everyone his own, or of administering, because it administers all things either by commanding or forbidding.

Since that time, the ten commandments was given by Moses. Those books of Moses the Pentateuch containing the law. Luke 24: 44; Acts 13: 15; Gal. 4: 21. For the law was given by Moses, but grace and truth came by Jesus Christ. Ex. 20: 1-17; Deut. 5: 1-27; Deut. 18: 15-19. For what the law could not do, in that it was weak through the flesh, God sending His own Son in the likeness of sinful flesh, and for sin, condemned sin in the flesh: That the righteousness of the law might be fulfilled in us, who walk not after the flesh, but after the spirit, Rom. 8: 3-4.

The scripture hath concluded all under sin, that the promise by the faith of Jesus Christ might be given to them that believe. But before faith came, we were kept under the law, shut up unto the faith which should afterwards be revealed. Wherefore the law was our schoolmaster to bring us unto Christ, that we might be justified (declared righteous) by faith.

But (however or nevertheless), after that faith is come, we are no longer under a schoolmaster. For as many of you as have been baptized into Christ have put on Christ, Gal. 3: 22-27. For ye are all the children of God by faith in Christ Jesus.

The schoolmaster or the law, the trustworthy servant slave, delivers us into the hand of Christ. So that in Christ's school we might be made right with God through faith. Once faith had come, we no longer need any such servant anymore. Already, here and now, being now justified by Christ's blood, we shall be saved from wrath (from the judgment of God) through Christ, Rom. 5: 9; 1 Thess. 1: 10.

For until ('till the time that) the law sin was in the world: However, sin is not imputed when there is no law. See Heb. 8: 7-13; John 12: 45-50. Nevertheless death reigned from Adam to Moses (until Christ's death, Rom. 3: 25; Eph. 2: 13), even over them that had not sinned after the similitude or likeness of Adam's transgression, who was the figure of Him (Christ) that was to come, Rom. 5: 13-14.

Even though the whole human race were not with Adam and Eve, our first parents in the garden of Eden, when they sinned. But we inherited their sins because of the natural laws of nature, in that, we are flesh and blood, of God's earthly creation.

Man's quest or pursuit for knowledge which he sought after inappropriately in the garden of Eden, the fruit they both had eaten, from the forbidden tree of knowledge of good and evil, brought upon us a dual nature of good and evil. Mankind is like a tree which either bears good or evil fruit. See Mt. 7: 15-20; Mt. 12: 30-33;

The Spirit of God must hold first place in our lives in all things: Apostle Paul had acknowledged in him that the nature of sin was still existing although he was born again. See Gal. 2: 15-19, 20-21; Gal. 3: 17-27. For he wrote: For we know that the law is spiritual: But I am carnal (flesh and blood), sold under sin, (sold into sin's slavery). For that which I do I allow not: For what I would, that do I not; but what I hate, that do I. If then I do that which I would not, I consent unto the law that it is good. Now then it is no more I that do it, but sin that dwelleth in me for I know that in me (that is, in my flesh), dwelleth no good thing: For to will is present with me; but how to perform that which is good I find not, Rom. 7: 14-18. That was why Jesus Christ the son of man had taken no credit to himself, but gave all credit to the Father (Spirit) that dwelleth in Him. Though He had no earthly connection (John 1: 13).

Jesus in giving us an example to follow, showed that the Spirit of God must have complete control over the flesh: For the life and works from within to be good. Either (we) make the tree good, and his fruit good; or else make the tree corrupt, and his fruit corrupt: For the tree is known by his fruit, Mt. 7: 33. Our critical perception of anyone should be the revealed truth of the spirit from an honest heart as proclaimed by Jesus. Mt. 12: 25-37.

Man's first opportunity to receive spiritual knowledge corporately, was to Israel after they were delivered from Egypt by God by the leadership of Moses, after the fall of man in the garden of Eden. This came about by the giving of the law to Israel. See Ex. 20: 1-17; Deut. 5: 1-27.

The next step of spiritual knowledge was through the Mosaic law to reveal to mankind his characteristics of the inner self of fallen man. As apostle Paul tells us; By the deeds of the law there shall no flesh be justified in God's sight: For by the law is the knowledge of sin, Rom. 3: 20. Having outlined the purpose of the law the apostle asked; What shall we say then? Is the law sin? God forbid. Nay, he replied: I had not known sin, but by the law: For I had not known lust, except the law had said, Thou shalt not covet.

But sin, taking occasion by the commandment, wrought in Paul all manner of concupiscence (lust). For without the law sin was dead. For I was alive without the law once: But when the commandment came, sin revived, and I died. And the commandment, which was ordained to life. Paul found to be unto death. For sin taking occasion (got the opportunity) by the commandment, deceived him, and by it slew him. Wherefore the law is holy, and the commandment holy, and just, and good.

Paul asked again. Was then that which is good made death unto him? God forbid. But sin, that it might appear sin, working death in him by that which is good: That the commandment might become exceeding sinful, Rom. 7: 7-13. The law is intolerant to sin, therefore, in order that sin in us might be recognized as sin, the law produced death though, it was good. Because the law worketh (bringeth) wrath: For where no law is, there is no transgression. Rom. 4: 15.

CHAPTER 7

The guaranteed Words of Jesus:

Jesus, in His guaranteed Words to His disciples, declared to them saying: Verily I say unto you, that ye which have followed Me, in the regeneration when the Son of Man shall sit in the throne of His glory, ye also shall sit upon twelve thrones, judging the twelve tribes of Israel, Mt. 19: 28. The regeneration refers to the restoration of the soul. The result of this new birth spoken of by Jesus which happens at conversion, when the individual is born again. John 3: 3-5, The blood of Jesus applied to the soul at the baptism of the convert, it does the washing or the cleansing of the individual, and the baptism by the Holy Ghost which is the Spirit of God, forms the linkages to complete the regeneration. Only by this process by faith in the name of Jesus can anyone be saved to obtain salvation, (Acts 4: 12).

The factors to accomplish the redemption of the soul of mankind is both spiritual and physical in that, it was the divine thought of the Almighty God to restore the lost image of man, made in the image of God. Then the worthiness of the redeemer had to be contemplated and implemented by his obedience unto the death on the cross by the giving of His life as required by God as the substitute for falling man which could not be found on earth nor in heaven. Rev. 5: 1-5; Heb. 2: 9-14; Heb. 10: 4-10.

Hence the grace of God in conjunction with God's love and mercy was the pivot to effect this great act of the redemption of the soul of man and ultimately the eternal salvation wrought by Christ Jesus. The Psalmist declared: None of them can by any means redeem his brother, nor give to God a ransom for him: For the redemption of their soul is precious, and it ceaseth forever. Ps. 49: 7-8.

The soul of man is described as precious. It is the most important part of man, because the soul is of great value or worth, being the inner-being of the human person. The soul is the spiritual and immortal part of man, which is immaterial and spiritual that inhabits the body. The soul is the moral and emotional part of man's nature; The seat of the sentiments or feelings; the soul is the spiritual being with a disembodied spirit. It is that part in man that gives him courage to be dauntless and strong in spirit. Without the soul the body is lifeless.

The keeping of our souls is the most valuable and essential thing in man to please God. Which the born again person can accomplish through Christ Jesus, who has given us the victory over the devil at Calvary.

The keeping of the soul is imperative for the words of Jesus clearly state: For what is a man profited if he shall gain the whole world, and lose his own soul? Or what shall a man give in exchange for his soul? Mt. 16: 26.

The imminent return of Jesus dictates that we keep our souls pure and steadfast. See I Thess. 3: 6-13; 1 Cor. 15: 49-58. For the son of man shall come in the glory (honour) of his Father (the Spirit) with His angels, and then He shall reward every man according to his works, Mt. 16: 27.

The blood of Christ, the cleansing fountain and the antidote for sin's removal and the Spirit of God justifies us as the children of God. This combination of blood and the Spirit of Christ Jesus forms the defence and suste-nance of the soul. These are the anchors of the soul of mankind.

CHAPTER 8

The unfolding of the wisdom of God:

This unfolding is the bringing to an end the body of sins by God through Christ Jesus, whom the Apostle Paul called: The great God and our Saviour, (Titus 2: 13) the Almighty. By His wisdom He veiled the Spirit, that is, Himself, by taking upon Himself, humanity, the human body, (Mt. 1: 20; Luke 1: 35) to put on the veil or covering of the Spirit, clothed Himself in humanity (John 13: 3; Heb. 10: 5; Heb. 2: 14; Heb. 9: 13-14); 1 Tim. 3: 16). As the writer of the Hebrews tells us: For so much then as the children are partakers of flesh and blood, Jesus also Himself likewise took part of the same; that through death He might destroy him that had the power of death, that is the devil.; And deliver them who through fear of death were all their lifetime subject to bondage, Heb. 2: 14-15 See 1 Cor. 15: 52-57.

For in him dwelleth all the fullness of the Godhead (divine nature) bodily, for as God in Spirit, He became man. Thus, His incarnation in the likeness of man, John 1: 14. And we are complete in Him, that is, Christ, which is the head of all principality and power: (in the heavenlies) In whom (Christ) we are circumcised with the circumcision made without hands, in putting off the body of sins of the flesh by the circumcision of Christ: See Rom. 6: 6; Rom. 2: 28-29. Buried with Christ in baptism, wherein also we are risen with Him through the faith of the operation of God (in baptism, symbolizing His death) who hath raised Him from the dead. Col. 2: 9-12.

The apostle Peter declared: For Christ also hath suffered (put to death) for our sins, the just (Christ) for mankind the unjust, that He might bring us to God, being put to death in the (His) flesh, but quickened (remained alive) by the Spirit.: By which also He went and preached unto the spirits (of the just) in prison (that was held in captive by the power of the devil): See Heb. 2: 14; Eph. 4: 8-11. There Jesus went and entered the strong man's house, bound him, and took away the keys of hell and of death. See Mt. 12: 29; Rev. 1: 18. And declared: I am He that liveth, and was dead (in body); and behold, I am alive forever more, Amen; and have the keys (authority) of hell and of death, Rev. 1: 18.

Apostle Peter tells us: For this cause was the Gospel preached also to them that are dead, that they might be judged according to men in the flesh, but live according to God, in the Spirit, 1 Pet. 4: 6. See 1 Pet. 3: 19 -20. God the Father which is the Spirit of God, by His great wisdom, saw the need to redeem His earthly creatures, whom He made in His own image (character) and after His likeness, which means: His similitude or image. Wherefore Jesus was made flesh in the likeness of man in order to restore and reconcile His image that was lost.

Therefore God veiled Himself by assuming a body for the covering of the Spirit, of Himself, in the person of Christ (Mt. 1: 20; Luke 1: 35; 1 Tim. 3: 16; Heb. 1: 1-3; Heb. 10: 5; Rom 1: 1-4; John 1: 14; John 14: 8-11), to redeem us back to God, through His death. See Phil. 2: 5-11. So that eternal life could be regained in us. Thus, on this gracious redemptive act by such great expression of love, he took our sins on the cross, where He was nailed and took upon Himself our curse and became a curse for us. See John 3: 14-18.

As it is written, Christ hath redeemed us from the curse of the law, being made for us (Mankind): For it is written, cursed is every one that hangeth on a tree: Gal. 3: 13. That the blessing of Abraham might come on the Gentiles (the nations of the world) through Jesus Christ (Eph. 2: 11-18): That we might receive the promise of the Spirit through faith, Gal. 3: 13-14.

Christ made Himself void of the Spirit of God, by His obedience to die for us to fulfill God's will and love for mankind. See Rom. 5: 7-10. Christ Jesus gave of Himself, and was taken to Golgotha and crucified: Mt. 27: 33-37, 45-50. Jesus in yielding up the spirit of God from His body, yielded up His life, and thereby made the greatest sacrifice in separating His body from the Father, the Spirit of God, thus he cried, my God, my God, why hast thou forsaken me? Mt.27: 46 (Ps. 22:1). In yielding up the Ghost (Spirit) He yielded Himself to God in obedience as an offering for sin, whereby he pleased God. See Isa. 53: 10-11. See John 8:29; John 6:38.

The Sons of God shall always be led by the Spirit of God

As Paul tells us: For as many as are led by the Spirit of God, they are the sons (children) of God. For we have not received the Spirit of bondage again to fear (Heb 2: 14-15; 2 Tim. 1: 7); but we have the spirit of adoption, whereby we cry, Abba Father.

The spirit itself beareth witness with our spirit, that we are the children of God. And if children, then heirs, heirs of God, and joint-heirs with Christ; If so be that we suffer with Him, that we may be also glorified together, Rom. 8: 14-17. For if we have been planted (buried in baptism) together in the likeness of His death, we shall be also in the likeness of His resurrection: See Gal. 5: 24:; Gal. 2: 20; Rom. 13: 13-14. Knowing this, that our old man is crucified with Him, that the body of sin might be destroyed, that henceforth we should not serve sin.

Now if we be dead with Christ, we believe that we shall also live with Him, Rom. 6: 5-8.

CHAPTER 9

Serving God with the mind of Christ

Holding forth the word of life, in obedience to the law of the spirit of life in Christ Jesus, which is the third or final phase of the law given to the church to serve in newness of spirit, with the mind of Christ, to vanquish (overcome) the flesh which goes hand in hand with the law of sin. See 1 Cor. 15: 56; Rom. 7: 6; Rom. 8: 2; Rom. 7: 25; Phil. 2: 5, 16.

The whole duty of the regeneration (born again) man is to fear God, and holding forth or going forward with the word of life which represents Christ Jesus the spirit of life. By whom we were chosen according to the foreknowledge of God the Father, through sanctification of the spirit, unto obedience and sprinkling (sacrificing) of the blood or physical life of Jesus Christ, to save us by His grace and restoring our peace with God.

This third and final phase of the establishment of the law or rule of the spirit of life in Christ Jesus hath made us free from the law of sin and death which was weak through the flesh (body), as Paul by the wisdom of God unfold in Rom. 7: 5-6, 15-24; Rom. 8: 3; Gal. 5: 19-21; which manifest itself from the garden of Eden, by Adam and Eve, and to Israel from Mount Sanai. Which the apostle says: Wherefore, as by one man sin entered into the world, and death by sin and so death passed upon all men, for that all have sinned: For until the law, sin was in the world: But sin is not imputed when there is no law.

The greatest victory to be won is the victory over the flesh by the Spirit of Christ. Christ Jesus demonstrated this victory by the giving (sacrificing) of His body on the cross and thereby triumphing in the spirit. The veiling or covering of the spirit of Christ (1 Pet. 1:

11) with humanity, in human body was preordained (Eph. 1: 4-9). For the redemption of the soul (Ps. 49: 8) of mankind and to bruise or crush Satan's head (Gen. 3; 15; Rom. 16: 20; Heb. 2: 14; Col. 2: 14-15), by the giving of His life on the cross, Mt. 27: 45-50.

The purpose of the cross is to mortify the flesh (put to death) the body of sin, which brought the downfall of our first earthly parents. Therefore it was the veiling of the body of Christ and the willingness to put His body to death through suffering that brought Christ victory and our deliverance and thereby the victory of the Spirit of God, over evil, sin and death.

For what is a man profited, if he shall gain the whole world, and lose his own soul? Or what shall a man give in exchange for his soul? For the son of man shall come in the glory of the Father with His angels; and then he shall reward every man according to his works, Mt. 16: 21-27.

Following the example of Christ, we shall save our souls, and obtain the reward of good works. See Rev, 20: 12; Rom. 2: 6; Rom. 14: 12; 2 Cor. 5: 10. Apostle Paul in his exhortation to the Philippians saints wrote: Let this mind be in you which was also in Christ Jesus: Who, being in the form (the essential) form which can be made visible to the eye) of God, thought it not robbery to be equal (the being of an equality) with God: But made himself of no reputation (he emptied himself), and took upon him the form of a servant (making himself void of the glory and his deity, the Godhead), and was made in the likeness of men: And being found in fashion (appearance) as a man, he humbled (abased) himself (2 Cor. 11: 7), and became obedient unto death (Heb. 5: 7-8), even the death of the cross. Wherefore God also hath highly exalted him (has given him the highest place, John 12: 24, 32; John 17: 1), and given him a name which is above every name, Phil. 2: 5-9.

CHAPTER 10

Lord Jesus the exalted name, the only saving name:

Lord Jesus the exalted name given by the angel Gabriel, is the only saving name: Mt. 1: 18-21; Like 1:26-35.

The Lord Jesus is the rock, the sure and solid foundation on whom to begin the building of our spiritual life, by our faith in his heavenly name, which the believer will demonstrate is firm conviction, confidence and complete trust by baptism in His name. The Lord Jesus declared to all mankind. "I am the way, the truth and the life: No man cometh to the Father, but by me." John 14: 6. In that, Jesus is the way into the holiest: Heb. 10: 19-23; Heb. 9: 8); the gospel of Jesus Christ is the truth of God's word, and believing in His words with continuity will make us true disciples indeed.

Then we shall know the truth, about Jesus, and the truth, which is Christ shall make us free, John 8: 31-32. For sin shall not have dominion over us, when we are in Christ: For we are not under the law (anymore), but under grace, hence we are free from the law of sin and death. Being then made free from sin, (since we are save), we become servants of righteousness. Therefore, now being made free from sin, and become servants to God, we have our fruit unto holiness, and the end (shall be) everlasting life. See Rom. 6: 14, 18, 22.

To make Jesus our only choice, is to choose life. For the word of God tells us: In Him (Jesus) was life (eternal); and the life (John 8: 12) was the light of men, (John 1: 4). To lead us into His kingdom, all who will obey Him. Water baptism in His name is fulfilling all righteousness. Mt. 3: 13-15; Acts 2: 37-39. Jesus declared to His disciples that repentance and remission of sins should be preached in His name among all nations, beginning at Jerusalem, Luke 24: 47.

Chapter 11

The Testimony of Jesus is the Spirit of prophecy

The apostle John wrote: I am thy fellow servant, and of thy brethren that have the testimony or the record of Jesus: Worship God, for the testimony of Jesus is the Spirit of Prophecy.

The testimony of Jesus is the truth of God's Word: For my thoughts are not your thoughts, neither are your ways my ways, saith the Lord. For as the heavens are higher than the earth, so are my ways higher than your ways, and my thoughts than your thoughts. For as the rain cometh down, and the snow from heaven, and returneth not thither, but watereth the earth, and maketh it bring forth and bud, that it may give seed to the sower, and bread to the eater: So shall my word be that goeth forth out of my mouth. It shall not return unto me void (empty), but it shall accomplish that which I please, and it shall prosper in the thing whereto I sent it. For ye shall go out with joy, and be led forth with peace: The mountains and the hills shall break forth before you into singing, and all the trees of the field shall clap their hands, Isa. 55: 8-11.
This was God's response concerning Israel that had hardened themselves against God's prophecy from the mouth of Isaiah the prophet, See Isa. 55: 1-7. An invitation to all to come and partake of God's grace freely: This prophecy points to the coming of Christ Jesus and His authority to save sinners.

CHAPTER 12

The Lord's purpose for His call to the Nations and to Israel

The chosen ones are the called out ones to be conformed to the image of Christ, through the message of the cross, to possess the mind of Christ, by putting to death the life of the flesh, and to think Christ-like and walk as He walked, leaving an example for us to follow: Therefore the message of the cross of Christ is the only thing that will transform us from our earthly lifestyle: Thus, the Lord Jesus counsels the called out: Take my yoke (submitting to the authority of Christ) upon us, and learn of Him; For Christ is meek and lowly in heart: And we shall find rest unto our souls. For His yoke is easy, and His burden is light, Mt. 11: 29-30. The Word of God, is the yoke that the believers shared with God throughout our life to hold us to God.

Apostle John wrote: Hereby we do know that we know Him, if we keep His commandments (Words). He that saith, I know Him, and keepeth not His commandments, is a liar, and the truth is not in him. But whoso keepeth His Word, in him verily is the love of God perfected: Hereby know we that we are in Him. He that saith he abideth in Him ought himself also so to walk even as He walked, 1 John 2: 3-6.

Apostle Peter says: This is thankworthy if a man for conscience toward God endures grief, suffering wrongfully. For what glory is it, if, when ye be buffeted for our faults, ye shall take it patiently? But if, when ye do well, and suffer for it, ye take it patiently, this is acceptable with God. For even hereunto were ye called: Because Christ also suffered for us, leaving us an example, that we should follow His steps: Who did no sin, neither was guile found in his mouth: Who, when he was reviled, reviled not again; When he suffered, he threatened not; but committed himself to him that judgeth righteously: Who his own self bore our sins in his own body on the tree, that we, being dead to sins, should live unto righteousness: By whose stripes we were healed. For we were as sheep going astray; but are now returned unto the Shepherd and Bishop of our souls, 1 Pet. 2: 19-25. Christ has shown us that as the son of man he committed his cause to the spirit exclusively to defeat the flesh.

CHAPTER 13

God in Jesus Christ the unique One:

The apostle Paul teaches the church of the unique oneness of Christ, asserts: To wit (that is), that God was in Christ, reconciling the world unto Himself, not imputing their trespasses unto them; and hath committed (put in us) or unto us the word of reconciliation.

Now then we are ambassadors for Christ, as though God did beseech you by us (the Apostles): Therefore they proclaimed: We pray you in Christ's stead, be ye reconciled to God. For He hath made him to be sin for us, who knew no sin, that ye might be made the righteousness of God in him, 2 Cor. 5: 19-21.

God has restored friendship through reconciliation by Christ removing the enmity and making peace through His blood. Thereby declaring His great love for us. John 3: 14-17; Rom 5: 7-10.

No man hath seen God at any time:

Therefore on this account of fact coming from the mouth of the Son of God, we should earnestly yield to all that He commands in the spirit of love as He reveals God's righteous requirements to the body of Christ, which is the church. The Word of God unfolds: No man hath seen God at any time (in all His essence); the only begotten Son, which is in the bosom of the Father, that is, Jesus proceeded forth and came from God (John 8: 42; John 5: 43; Luke 1; 35; Mt. 1; 19-21), He hath declared Him, See John 1: 18.

Obedience to His commands is the sure foundation of truth:

Luke 6: 47-48. Apostle Paul exhorts: Wherefore, my beloved, as ye have always obeyed, not as in my presence only, but now much more in my absence, work out your (our) own salvation with fear and trembling. For it is God which worketh in you both to will (desire) and to do (accomplish) of His good pleasure.

Murmurings and disputings are forbidden:

We are expected to do all things without murmurings and disputings: 1 Cor. 10: 10; Rom. 14: 1-3. That we may be blameless and harmless (innocent), the sons of God, without rebuke, in the midst of a crooked (twisted) and perverse or perverted nation, among whom we should shine as lights in the world, Phil. 2: 12-15.

As we must go forth holding or offering the word of life. That we may rejoice in the day of Christ, that we have not run in vain, neither labored in vain, Phil. 2: 16.

CHAPTER 14

Believing the gospel of Christ brings, the righteousness which is of God by faith:

The theme of the entire gospel is Jesus Christ, therefore believing in Him and accepting His authority is the only way for a victorious life. Jesus declared after the resurrection as He met with His disciples, He told them: All power is given unto me in heaven and in earth. Go ye therefore, and teach all nations, baptizing them in the name of the Father, and of the Son, and of the Holy Ghost. Teaching them to observe all things whatsoever I have commanded you: And, lo, I am with you always, even unto the end of the world.

The understanding of how the baptism was to be performed, explained in: Luke 24: 45-47; taken from Mt. 28: 19; and accomplished in (Acts 2: 36-41; Acts 8; 14-17; Acts 10: 44-48; Acts 16: 14-15; Acts 19: 1-7); Acts 4: 12; Col. 3: 17; Gal 1; 8; Eph. 4: 5-6; Acts 3: 20-23;Mk 16: 14-20. *The scriptures given outside the brackets from Acts 4: 12 shows the reason.* In baptizing according to the commands of Jesus, all righteousness is fulfilled, (Mt. 3: 14-15), following he will give the Holy Ghost to all who obey Him. Acts 5: 32. See Acts 2: 4; Acts 10: 44; John 4: 14; John 7: 37-38.

The beginning of righteousness is faith, (Rom. 4: 5 -6). Baptism is faith by works, which is the fulfillment of righteousness, Mt. 3: 13-17. As Paul testified: For I am not ashamed of the gospel of Christ: For it is the power of God unto salvation; To the Jew first, and also to the Greek. For therein is the righteousness of God revealed from faith to faith: As it is written, the just shall live by faith, Rom. 1; 16-17.

Therefore having now become a partaker of the

righteousness of God which is by the faith of Jesus Christ which is unto all and upon all them that believe: For there is no difference: For all have sinned, and come short of the Glory of God. Being justified freely by His grace through the redemption that is in Christ Jesus: Whom God hath set forth or foreordained to be a propitiation through faith in His blood, to declare His righteousness for the remission of sins that are past, through the forbearance of God. To declare I say at this time His righteousness: That He might be just, and the justifier of him which believeth in Jesus, Rom. 3: 22-26.

CHAPTER 15

Jesus the author and finisher of our faith, in whom God first trusted:

The Lord Jesus whom God hath foreordained to be the propitiation or the atoning sacrifice through our faith in His blood, for the covering of the sins from Adam to Moses that are past, since Calvary, because of the forbearance of God, to demonstrate His righteousness. See Acts 17: 13-15, 29-30; Acts 13: 38-39. To declare at this time His righteousness: For by grace are we saved through faith, that He might be just (righteous) and the justifier of him (the believer), which believeth in Jesus, Rom. 3: 22-26. See Rom. 2; 2-4; Rom. 3: 25.

The forbearance and longsuffering in His patience is the manifestation of the goodness of God which leadeth to repentance. Israel was exhorted to believe in the Lord their God: 2 Chr. 20: 20-27. Jehoshaphat had exhorted Judah and the inhabitants of Jerusalem; to believe in the Lord their God, so that they would be established; and believe in their prophets given to them by God, for so shall they prosper.

God first had set the example to trust Jesus for us to follow: According as He hath chosen us in Him before the foundation of the world, that we should be holy and without blame before Him in love.: Having predestined us unto the adoption of children by Jesus Christ to Himself, according to the good pleasure of His will. To the praise of the glory of His Grace (own self), wherein He hath made us accepted in the beloved. Eph. 1: 4-6. That we should be to the praise of His glory, who first trusted in Christ. In whom we also trusted, after that we heard the word of truth, the gospel of our salvation: In whom also after that we believed, we were sealed with that holy spirit of promise. Which is the earnest of our inheritance until the redemption of the (our) purchased possession, unto the praise of His glory (own self), Eph. 1: 12-14.

Jesus the gift of God to the world.

Every good gift and every perfect gift is from above, and cometh down from the Father of lights, with whom is no variableness, neither shadow of turning. Of His own will begat He us with the word of truth, that we should be a kind of first fruit of His creatures, Jas. 1: 17-18.

Born again believers are the first fruits of the creatures of Christ: Rev. 14: 4. See Jas. 1: 18; John 1: 13; John 3: 3; 1 Cor 4: 15-16; 1 Pet. 1: 22-23.

The prophecy concerning Christ:

The prophet Isaiah proclaimed: "The Lord God hath opened my ear, and I was not rebellious, neither turned away back". The prophet foreseen Christ in his submission to God's will on his way to Golgotha being obedient unto death. Thus he prophesied of Him saying: I was not rebellious (disobedient), neither turned away back. Mt. 26: 39.

The bible teaches while He had the last supper with His disciples after He had completed, He went unto a place called Gethsemane, and saith unto His disciples, sit ye here, while I go and pray yonder. And He took with Him Peter and the two sons of Zebedee, and began to be sorrowful and very heavy.

Then saith He unto them, my soul is exceeding sorrowful, even unto death: Tarry (wait) ye here, and watch with me. And He went a little farther, and fell on His face, and prayed, saying: Oh my Father, if it be possible, let this cup pass from me: *The cup He referred to is the cross, that He came to experience His death on.* And He declared willingly: Nevertheless, not as I will, but as Thou wilt, Mt. 26: 39. See Isa. 50: 5. I gave my back to the smiters (Mt. 26: 67; Mt. 27: 26; John 18: 22), and my cheeks to them that plucked off the hair: I hid not my face from shame and spitting. Mt. 26: 67.

For the Lord God will help me: Therefore shall I not be confounded: Therefore have I set my face like a flint, and I know that I shall not be ashamed. This is in respect of his servant who will stand for God, shall not be ashamed. (Isa. 50: 6-7. See Rom. 1: 13-17). He is near that justifieth (Rom. 8: 32-34) me, who will contend with me? Let us stand together: Who is mine adversary? Let him come near to me.   Behold, the Lord God will help me. Who is he that shall condemn me? (Rom. 8: 33-34). Lo, they shall wax old as a garment; the moth shall eat them up, (1 Pet. 1: 24-25).

Who is among you that feareth the Lord, that obeyeth the voice of his servant, that walketh in darkness, (Ps. 23:4) and hath no light? Let him trust in the name of the Lord, and stay upon his God, Isa. 50: 5-10. The body of Christ will raise their banner: Symbolizing the Lord's victory in His salvation, and in the name of our God we will set (erect) up our banner: The Lord fulfills all thy petitions (prayers). Now know I that the Lord saveth His anointed; He will hear him from His holy heaven with the saving strength of His right hand, (Isa. 59: 16-17). Some trust in chariots, and some in horses: Ex. 14: 26-31. But we will remember the name of the Lord our God, Ps. 20: 5 -7 See John 20: 26-30.

The Lord Jesus, the beginner and the finisher of the faith, was tested in all points yet without sin. The Word of God gives us firm assurance of Jesus in whom God first trusted, to fulfill His divine will, of which He was victorious. Seeing then that we have a great high priest, that is passed into the heavens, Jesus the Son of God, let us hold fast our profession. For we have not a great high priest which cannot be touched (reached) with the feeling of our infirmities; but was in all points tempted like as we are, yet without sin. Let us therefore come boldly unto the throne of grace, that we may obtain mercy, and find grace to help in time of need. Heb. 4: 14-16.

Since Christ Jesus came in the flesh and was   human, just as we are and have been through all human trials and was victorious in all His experiences, then it is fitting for us to trust Him for all our concerns: Apostle Paul in comparing his life in the law, and his life in Christ Jesus, when he came in contact with Jesus, says: He was circumcised the eighth day, of the stock of Israel, of the tribe of Benjamin, an Hebrew of the Hebrews; as touching the law a Pharisee; Concerning zeal, persecuting the church; touching the righteousness which is in the law, blameless.

But what things were gain to me, those I counted loss for Christ. Yea doubtless, and I count all things but loss for the excellency of the knowledge of Christ Jesus my Lord: For whom I have suffered the loss of all things, and do count them but dung. That I may win Christ. "And be found in Him, not having mine own righteousness, which is of the law", but that which is through the faith of Christ, the righteousness which is of God by faith: That I may know Him, and the power of His resurrection, and the 54 fellowship of His sufferings, being made conformable unto His death, Phil. 3: 5-10.

Paul's first call by Jesus while on the journey to Damascus and the heavenly glory that shone round about Him caused him to get an insight of the fullness of the heavenly glory with Christ. Which he was not willing to lose sight of, therefore he gave up all that he had obtained by the law because in his summing up of the law it was not worthy to be compared with the glory of heaven with Christ on the throne as King of kings and Lord of lords, to be revealed. In his pursuit to win Christ, to know Him and to experience the power of His resurrection and what is the fellowship of His sufferings, he was willing to surrender all to Christ, and to be made conformable unto His death.

This was the choice of Paul: If by any means he might attain unto the resurrection of the dead. He thought that would be the greatest blessing to be achieved in Jesus Christ.

CHAPTER 16

The mystery of the Gospel revealed to Paul:

He told the church of the Ephesians, how that by revelation He made known unto him the mystery which was hid. Whereby, when they read, they may understand His knowledge in the mystery of Christ. Which in other ages was not made known unto the sons of men, as it is now revealed unto His holy apostles and prophets by the Spirit. That the Gentiles should be fellow heirs, and of the same body, and partakers of His promise in Christ by the gospel:

The gospel message of Jesus Christ can take us into the highest realm of His spiritual kingdom which we should aspire to attain. Whereof Paul was made a minister according to the gift of the grace of God given unto him by the effectual working of his power, by the Word and Spirit of God.

Unto me, (Paul recalled his past life, the damage he had done to the church. Who was before a blasphemer, and a persecutor and injurious: 1Tim: 1: 13). "Who am less than the least of all saints, is this grace (ministry) given, that I should preach among the Gentiles or Nations the unsearchable riches of Christ. The Spirit of God within the body of Christ, reveals what is the mind of God, comes by the revelation of Christ. And to make all men see (understand) what is the fellowship (partnership) of the hidden secret in God, which from the beginning of the world hath been hid in God, who created all things by Jesus Christ, Eph. 3: 5-9. The church through Paul revealed to angels (principalities and powers, in the heavenlies) the manifold wisdom of God. To the intent (intention or disclosure) that now unto the principalities and powers in heavenly places might be known by the church the manifold wisdom of God, Eph. 5: 5-10. The unsearchable riches of Christ, can only be reached in the sphere of the gospel, hid in God in Christ in whom all blessings exist or consist. Col. 1: 13-17.

Christ the Power of God and the Wisdom of God:

But we (the Apostles and Prophets) preached Christ crucified, unto the Jews (the first fruit of Israel) a stumbling block, and unto the Greeks (Intelligensia) foolishness; but unto them which are called, both Jews and Greeks (the first fruit of Christ, the born again), Christ the power of God, and the wisdom of God, 1 Cor. 1: 23-24.

Now to Him (God) that is of power to stablish you (anyone) according to the gospel, and the preaching of Jesus Christ, according to the revelation of the mystery, which was kept secret since the world began, but now is made manifest, and by the scriptures of the prophets, according to the commandment of the everlasting God, made known to all nations for the obedience of faith, Rom. 16: 25-26.

For by grace are we saved through faith (the trust or confidence in Jesus); and that not of ourselves: It is the gift of God: Eph. 2: 8. For the grace (great favour) of God in Jesus Christ that bringeth salvation hath appeared to all men; teaching us that, denying, that is, refusing or reject-ing ungodliness and worldly lusts, we should live soberly, righteously and godly in this present world; looking for that blessed hope (Acts 24: 14-15), and the glorious appearing of the great God and our Saviour Jesus Christ; in whom dwellest all the fullness of the Godhead bodily. And we are complete in Him, which is the head of all principality and power, Col. 2: 9-10, who gave Himself for us, that He might redeem us (with His own blood) from all iniquity (lawlessness), and purify unto Himself a peculiar people, zealous of good works, Titus 2: 11-14.

CHAPTER 17

God's Proclamation fulfilled in Jesus Christ:

God's proclamation to Moses for keeping mercy for thousands, forgiving iniquity and transgression and sin, ... unto the third and to the fourth generation, accom-plished in Jesus. Ex. 34: 6-7.

The scripture teaches that the Lord called up Moses to come up to Mt. Sanai, to present himself there and God descend in the cloud and stood before him, proclaimed the name of the Lord. The Lord God, merciful and gracious, longsuffering (patient), and abundant in goodness and truth. Keeping mercy for thousands, forgiving iniquity (lawlessness), transgression and sin, accomplished by Christ Jesus in the new covenant.

And that will by no means clear the guilty; see Ex. 23: 7,21. The Lord forgives, but He expects us to forsake doing the wrong things continuously. See John 8: 1-11, 12. He keeps visiting the iniquity of the fathers (they never ceased) upon the children, and upon the children's children, unto the third and to the fourth generation, Ex. 34: 6 -7.

The prayer of Jerimiah to God:

Jeremiah prayed; Ah Lord God! Behold, Thou hast made the heaven and the earth by Thy great power and stretched out arm, and there is nothing too hard for Thee: Thou shewest lovingkindness unto thousands, and recompensed the iniquity of the fathers into the bosom of their children after them: The Great, the Mighty God, the Lord of Hosts, is His name. Great in counsel, and mighty in work: For Thine eyes are open upon all the ways of the sons of men: To give everyone according to his ways, and according to the fruit of his doings: Jer. 32: 17-19, 37-42, See Jer. 33: 7, 11, 25-26.

The promise of the new covenant
of keeping mercy foretold:

God is holy, which is the characteristics of His divine nature, which He manifests in His works, displayed towards His people and the nations of the world, to save us all.

Therefore, the apostle Paul in his analysis of God's Grace, exhorted the Ephesian saints to be of the same mind of Christ, saying: Let all bitterness, and wrath, and anger, and clamour, and evil speaking, be put away from us, with all malice: And be ye kind one to another, tender-hearted, forgiving one another, even as God for Christ's sake hath forgiven us, Eph. 4: 31-32.

The sins by succession or from generation to generation from the third to the fourth generation from our fathers, will be cleansed by the Blood of Christ, which is rendered propitious by His atoning sacrifice for the remission of sins: Apostle John says: If we say that we have no sin (inherit from Adam, which we became knowledgeable of, by the giving of the Mosaic law, and thereby all men became guilty), we deceive ourselves, and the truth is not in us. If we confess our sins (hidden in us by our Adamic nature in the flesh), He is faithful and just to forgive us our sins, and to cleanse us from all unrighteousness, 1 John 1: 8-9.

It is the power of the Blood of Christ that will cover us and free us by our faith in His name through conversion. Following which, if we walk in the Spirit we shall not fulfill the lusts of the flesh. The Gospel of Christ is the power of God to deliver fallen man unto salvation which gives everlasting life and happiness. This is the only recourse God has established to save mankind, if they will be obedient to the message of Jesus Christ, to restore the soul that was dead in trespasses and sin to spiritual life again that was lost in Adam.

Therefore the Gospel of Christ is the resuscitating life giving source that is offered by God to restore the spiritually dead soul to life again. The sacrifice of the life of Jesus in the flesh was the pouring out of His Blood to redeem the soul of mankind and to heal their sick soul.

The soul of unrepentant sinners
is sick and needs healing:

The repentant sinners are now saved by Christ Jesus: Who His own self borne our sins in His own body on the tree (cross), that we, being dead to sins, should live unto righteousness: By whose stripes we were healed. For we were as sheep going astray; but are now returned unto the shepherd and bishop of our souls. 1 Pet. 1: 24-25.

God's holy character and embodied in Jesus Christ, with His divine nature of holiness vested in Him, enabled Jesus to manifest the spirit of forbearance and longsuffering, which is patience, as He held back His wrath and anger against the failings of humanity, of continuous sin and in His patience endured the cross, so that we might be healed through Christ Jesus.

CHAPTER 18

Christ Jesus the suffering servant:

The prophet Isaiah, portrayed Christ as God's suffering servant, says: Behold, my servant shall deal prudently, he shall be exalted and extolled, and be very high. As many were astonished or appalled at thee; His visage was so marred more than any man, and His form more than the sons of men: So shall He sprinkle many nation; the kings shall shut their mouths at Him: For that which had not been told them shall they see; and that which they had not heard shall they consider, Isa. 52: 13-15.

The prophet proclaimed: Surely He hath borne our grief, and carried our sorrows: Yet we did esteem Him stricken, smitten of God, and afflicted. But He was wounded for our transgressions, He was bruised for our iniquities: The chastisement (chastening or punishment) of our peace (well-being) was upon Him; and with His stripes (bruise, black & blue) we are healed (made whole). Isa. 53: 4-5.

By the punishment Christ suffered for us, bruised until it was black and blue, we are made whole, covered by His Blood and are now in a state of wellness. Our souls are now healed completely by the sacrifice of the Apostle and High Priest of our profession, Christ Jesus.

We are commanded to take the Gospel
unto the uttermost part of the earth: Acts 1: 8.

The mandate of   Jesus to His disciples: That after the Holy Ghost is come upon us, we should be witness unto Him both in Jerusalem and in all Judea, and in Samaria, and unto the uttermost part of the earth (the four corners of the earth).

This command is mandatory according to our calling in the ministry of the Word of God. This special function of the believers, after they have been taught the principles of Christ and the doctrine of the church, which is the Body of Christ, still stands.

This was the example set by the apostles of Jesus and their co-workers. The call of Paul the apostle was to fulfill this important mandate, thus when he went to Thessalonica they entered the Synagogue of the Jews three Sabbath days to preach Christ to them, and reason with them out of the scriptures. Opening and alleging that Christ must needs have suffered, and risen again from the dead: And that Jesus, whom he preached unto them, is Christ.

Now when the rulers of the city understood that the apostles were there: They were told, "These that have turned the world upside down are come hither also". Such were the mandate and mindset of the early church to evangelize the world preaching Christ to them. Acts 17: 1-8.

The Bible teaches, after the Lord had risen from the dead, He appeared and had spoken unto them, He was received up into heaven, and sat on the right hand of God. And they (the disciples) went forth, and preached everywhere, the Lord working with them, and confirming the Word with signs following. Amen. See Mk. 16: 14-20.

This instruction by Jesus to the disciples of the early church was obeyed and proclaimed by the Apostles. But since the Apostles have died this important mandate of Christ to the church has reduced greatly, and we are now limiting the preaching of the gospel of Christ, to our individual assembly, mainly.

I am afraid this is not what the Lord Jesus commands us to do! We are in the last days the coming of the Lord Jesus is near at hand. The need to arise and take the Gospel to the uttermost part of the earth is now! Not just to preach by media, but going physically into all the earth as the Apostles! Let us arise and do it for Jesus!

Embracing the Name of Jesus and
The End Time Call:

This is an end time call and the Foundation of the Truth of God's Word, from His holy prophets, the apostles, and the believers, who have obtained (the same) like precious faith, with the apostles: Who were commissioned, for (through) the righteousness of God and our Saviour, Jesus Christ. Through preaching and teaching, from the beginning of the creation of man to this age (the end time), to return us back to God, through obedience to the heavenly call. See 2 Pet. 1: 1; Rom. 1: 12; 2 Cor. 4: 13; Eph. 4: 5; Titus 1: 4.

It is an "Apostolic Perspective", from the fall of man, to the sojourn in Egypt of Israel, to their exodus in the wilderness, the receiving of the commandments (Law), to the New Covenant authorized by Jesus Christ, to all the nations of the world, to be joint heirs with Christ Jesus in His Kingdom.

His words of the final embrace for all the nations of the world:

Jesus our Lord, proclaims: Behold, I come quickly. Hold that fast which thou hast, that no man take thy crown. Him that overcometh will I make a pillar in the temple of my God, and he shall go no more out: And I will write upon him the name of my God, and the name of the city of my God, which is new Jerusalem, which cometh down out of heaven from my God: And I will write upon him my new name, Rev. 3: 11-12. Amen

The Final Call to attain the Image of Christ:

The call to come to Christ is to conform to His image, manifesting His character in our everyday life in order to endure to the end and this is the goal we should aspire to attain, to be victorious.

Summary

This section gives a summary of the book entitled "The Foundation of Truth", which depicts the Creator as a Supreme Being and Sovereign Ruler of heaven above and the earth beneath where humans dwell.

It tells of the first husband and wife joined together by God in the garden of Eden, who became one flesh in God's announcement and failed in their pursuit to be wise as God. It shows the danger of deception and the importance of obedience.

The book highlights the call of Abraham from his Father's nativity to Canaan, the promised land. It tells of Abraham as the spiritual channel of righteousness by faith in God and the epitome of obedience, godly reverence in building an altar to offer sacrifice to God, and through whom the whole family of the earth is blessed, both Jews and Gentiles, through Christ Jesus, who came to earth as the seed of Abraham according to the flesh and called the Father of the Hebrews.

It shows the church, the body of Christ, known as the born again of this age, as the people of God and is likened to a building which hath foundation with Christ Jesus, the chief corner stone on whom the entire building is secured, and the Apostles referred to as the pillars and foundation of the truth the gospel of Christ, these formed the nucleus of the body of Christ called the church.

These apostles were entrusted with the responsibility to teach all nations with the truth of the gospel of Christ given to us through the epistles or letters sent to the churches. Hence the meaning: "The Foundation of Truth" understanding The Apostles Teaching.

The book touches all the facets of life that will cause or bring all humanity to Christ to be saved, that they may enter the Kingdom of God with Christ Jesus, at His return to gather His chosen, the elect, to the marriage supper of the lamb.

This book, The Foundation of Truth, with the subtitle: Adam and Eve in pursuit of the knowledge of good and evil to become wise as God. It's a treasure of incomparable value to have in every library to reflect on life where we are coming from and where we are going at the end of our physical journey on earth.

A resource hand book for all persons desirous of knowing about the Jesus name believers, that is, our concept in abstract ideas and the qualities we espouse as authorized by the apostles of Jesus Christ.

The aim of this book is to teach the doctrine of Christ and His apostles and to inspire all persons to be with Christ in His Kingdom.

About the Author

Wilfred Morais Brown is a Commissioned Justice of the Peace and Minister of Religion who resides with his family in Kingston, Jamaica, West Indies. He grew up in Stony Hill, St. Andrew, Jamaica, and his Christian life began in 1970 with the Church of God in Christ Jesus Apostolic.

He was ordained by the International Assembly of Apostolic Association Ministry in 2002 and has been a religious writer since 2003.Wilfred continues to live in Kingston, Jamaica with his wife of 42 years and their children and is heavily involved Christian Teaching, Restorative Justice and Child Rights Advocacy.

Notes

Notes

Notes

Notes

Notes